Trucks

Chris Oxlade

WAYLAND

First published in 2008 by Wayland

Copyright © Wayland 2008

Wayland
Hachette Children's Books
338 Euston Road
London NW1 3BH

Wayland Australia
Level 17/207 Kent Street
Sydney, NSW 2000

Senior Editor: Jennifer Schofield

Produced by Tall Tree Ltd
Editor: Rob Scott Colson
Designer: Darren Jordan
Consultant: Ben Russell

Oxlade, Chris
  Trucks. - (Machines inside out)
  1. Trucks - Juvenile literature
  I. Title
  629.2'24

ISBN: 978-0-7502-5324-6

Printed in China

Wayland is a division of Hachette Children's Books, an Hachette Livre UK company.

Acknowledgements
Cover Fernando Rodrigues/Dreamstime.com
6 John Van Straalen, 7t General Motors, 7b John Van Straalen,
8–9 Kevin Hulsey Illustration, Inc., 8 Paula Gent/Dreamstime.com,
9 Max Blain/Dreamstime.com, 10–11 Kevin Hulsey Illustration, Inc.,
12t Zoediak/Dreamstime.com, 12b Paul A. Souders/CORBIS,
13 H. Kent Sundling/MrTruck.net, 14–15 Dannyphoto80/
Dreamstime.com, 15 H. Kent Sundling/MrTruck.net,
16–17 Chrysler LLC. Dodge (the Dodge Ram's Head Logo are
trademarks of Chrysler LLC), 16 Nick Stubbs/Dreamstime.com,
17 H. Kent Sundling/MrTruck.net, 18 John Van Straalen,
19t David Freund/istockphoto, 19b Dreamstime.com,
20t Chris Scotti, 20b Stahlkocher/Wikipedia GNU,
21 Kevin Hulsey Illustration, Inc., 22 Jolin/Dreamstime.com,
23b Michael Emerson/Dreamstime.com,
23t David Monniaux/Creative Commons ShareAlike,
24 Walter Hodges/Brand X/Corbis, 25t John Van Straalen,
25b Frederic Pitchal/Sygma/Corbis, 26 Jack Mills/Dreamstime.com,
27b Elementalimaging/Dreamstime.com,
27t Thomas Mounsey/istockphoto

Contents

Trucks inside out

A truck is a complicated machine. Inside a truck, there are thousands of parts, from the heavy metal engine block to delicate electronic components that work the driver's instrument panel. This book explains how trucks work. It looks at large cargo trucks, such as the Peterbilt truck below, and smaller pick-up trucks, such as the Isuzu on page 8.

Driver's cab

Diesel engine

Radiator

Tractors and trailers

Trucks come in many shapes and sizes. The truck on these pages is called a tractor unit. Its job is to pull trailers, which are connected at the back. The tractor unit and trailer together are called an articulated truck.

Tractor unit

Trailer

Right-hand drive

For the United Kingdom and some other countries, such as Australia, trucks are built with the steering wheel on the right-hand side of the car, like this one. For most countries, the steering wheel is on the left. Other parts are in the same place.

TECH FACT

The largest trucks in the world are in Australia. They are called road trains because one tractor unit pulls up to four trailers, in the same way that a train locomotive pulls several carriages. The heaviest road trains weigh almost 200 tonnes (the same weight as 300 elephants).

Fuel tank

Engine compartment cover

Wheels

Truck structure

A truck needs a super-strong structure to support its weight and the weight of the cargo it carries. The main structure is called the chassis (say SHA-SEE). The chassis is a steel frame under the truck's body, which stretches from the front to the back. All the other parts of the truck are attached to the chassis.

Body

Rails and crossmembers

The chassis has two long lengths of steel called rails. There is one rail on each side of the truck. These are joined together by shorter pieces of steel, called crossmembers. There are holes in the rails and crossmembers for other parts to be bolted onto the chassis.

The fifth wheel

The tractor unit of an articulated truck has a connector on the back of its chassis. The connector is known as the fifth wheel. A large pin on the trailer slots into the fifth wheel. It locks into place so that the tractor can pull the trailer.

Fifth wheel

Trailer structure

The trailer of an articulated truck also has a chassis. Two long rails run from front to back, joined together by crossmembers. They support the weight of the cargo in the trailer. The wheels, legs and body of the trailer are attached to the chassis.

TECH FACT

A chassis is carefully designed to take the weight of the truck and its cargo. The rails and crossmembers inside a big cargo truck are wider, deeper and made of thicker steel than those in a pick-up truck. The larger chassis is stronger and stiffer, so it does not bend under the load.

Engine

I-TEC

Rail

Crossmember

Wheels and suspension

A truck's wheels spread its weight over the road. Two or four wheels are turned by the engine. Tyres grip the road so that the truck can turn corners, accelerate and brake safely. Suspension lets the wheels move up and down as the truck goes over bumps. The suspension keeps the tyres in contact with the road and stops the truck from bouncing up and down.

Shocks and springs

Each wheel is attached to the chassis by an arm that lets it move up and down. Springs on each arm support the chassis. Each wheel also has a shock absorber, which stops the spring becoming too squashed if the truck hits a large bump.

Shock absorber

Air suspension

Many trucks have air suspension. In these trucks, each wheel is attached to a rubber bag. The rubber bag is effectively a very strong balloon, and works just like a spring. The pressure of the air inside the bag can be adjusted to raise or lower the suspension.

TECH FACT

Tyres are filled with air. The air pressure must be just right to stop the tyres wearing out unevenly. Too much air and the centre of the tread wears down. Too little and the outsides of the tread wear down. Uneven wear can make a tyre burst or make the truck skid in the wet.

Spring

Shock absorber

-TEC

Truck tyres

A truck's tyres are made from rubber strengthened inside with thin layers of steel. Truck tyres are larger and stronger than car tyres because they must carry much more weight. The tyre tread pushes water away, letting the tyre grip a wet road.

Tyre

Wheel

Truck engines

Trucks need powerful engines to get moving and to pull heavy cargoes. Most trucks have diesel engines. These engines are more efficient and more powerful than petrol engines. But they are heavier. The fuel burns inside spaces called cylinders. The burning fuel pushes pistons along the cylinders. This movement turns the engine's crankshaft.

Engine arrangements

The engine on the opposite page is called an in-line six because it has six cylinders arranged in a straight line. This is the most common type of diesel truck engine, but smaller trucks may have in-line fours.

Under the bonnet

A truck's engine is often in front of and below the driver's cab, under the bonnet. The engine is attached to the front part of the chassis. On cabover trucks, the whole cab tips forwards to let an engineer work on the engine.

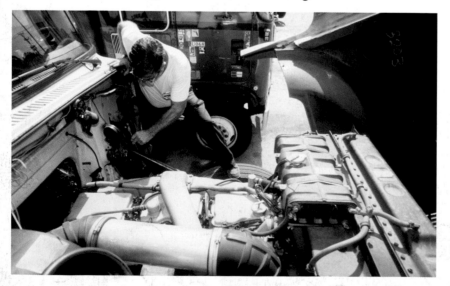

Lubrication

The metal parts of a truck engine are constantly moving against each other. Engine oil lets them move without rubbing and wearing out. This is called lubrication. The oil is pumped around by an oil pump, and kept clean by oil filters like these shown above.

Piston

Cylinder

Flywheel

Connecting rod

Crankshaft

TECH FACT

Truck engines are larger, heavier and far more powerful than car engines. A truck engine can weigh more than a tonne (heavier than a whole family car). The largest engines have a capacity of up to 16 litres – 10 times the size of a 1.6-litre car engine. An engine this size produces 10 times the power, too.

How the engine works

As a diesel engine runs, each cylinder follows a sequence of moves. This sequence is called the four-stroke cycle because each piston goes up and down its cylinder twice during the sequence. One valve opens to let air into the cylinder. Another opens to let exhaust gases out. The fuel is sprayed into the cylinder by a fuel injector.

Fuel injector

Piston

Timing
The valves must open and close at the right time, and the fuel must be injected at the right moment. The camshaft (see opposite) is turned by a belt from the crankshaft (above).

Intake stroke
Piston moves down.
Air sucked into cylinder.

Compression stroke
Piston moves up.
Air squeezed into top of cylinder, making it hot.

Camshafts and valves

Valves are holes in the top of a cylinder that can be open or closed. The intake valve opens during the intake stroke to let in air. The exhaust valve opens during the exhaust stroke to let exhaust gases out. The valves are opened by the cams on the spinning camshaft. They are closed again by springs.

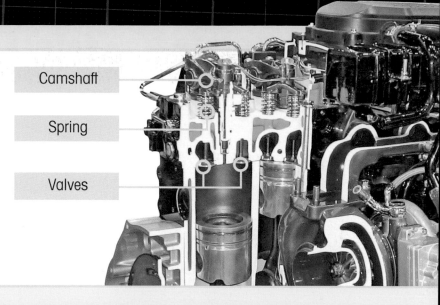

Camshaft

Spring

Valves

TECH FACT

In a diesel engine, the fuel ignites, or begins to burn, because the air in the cylinder is very hot. The air is hot because it is squeezed, or compressed, by the piston into a tiny space. This is why a diesel engine is also called a compression-ignition engine.

Power stroke
Fuel injected and explodes. Piston pushed down.

Exhaust stroke
Piston moves up. Exhaust gases pushed out.

Fuel and exhaust

A truck engine needs fuel to work. The fuel is stored in the fuel tank and burns in the cylinders. The fuel system moves the fuel from the tank to the cylinders in the engine. The system also supplies air to the engine, because the fuel cannot burn without air. The exhaust system removes waste gases left after the fuel burns.

Catalytic converter

Exhaust manifold

Air filters
A truck engine needs a lot of clean air in which to burn fuel. The air is sucked in from outside the truck through an air filter, which removes dirt from the air. Any dirt in the air would quickly clog up the engine's parts. There is a can-shaped air filter on the side of this truck.

TECH FACT

The exhaust gases flow along pipes to a box called a catalytic converter. There are special chemicals, called catalysts, inside the catalytic converter. These chemicals change harmful gases into less harmful gases. The new gases carry on along the exhaust pipe and out into the atmosphere.

The silencer

Blasts of exhaust gases come along the exhaust pipe from the engine. The silencer muffles the blasts. This stops the gases coming out of the exhaust pipe with a loud bang.

Turbocharging

The more air an engine can get into its cylinders, the more fuel it can burn, and so the more power it can produce. Large truck engines have a device called a turbocharger (or just 'turbo'). The turbo pumps air into the engine's cylinders, which makes the engine more powerful. The turbocharger is powered by exhaust gases coming from the cylinders.

Silencer

Exhaust pipe

Fuel tank

Turbocharger

Air intake

Cooling the engine

As an engine works, heat is made by the burning fuel and when the engine parts rub together. This makes parts of the engine very hot. They must be cooled to stop them getting too hot, which would make the engine seize up. The cooling system removes heat from the engine. It pumps water through the engine, which carries the heat away.

Pumping water

Water is pumped through spaces called ducts inside the engine block. The heat from the engine parts is transferred into the water. This cools the engine and heats up the water. The hot water then flows through the radiator, which cools it down again.

Radiator

Coolant hoses

Cooling water

The radiator is at the front of the truck. When the truck is moving, air flows over the radiator, cooling the water inside. When the truck is stationary, a fan blows air over the radiator.

TECH FACT

The cooling system is controlled by a device called a thermostat. When the engine temperature goes up, the thermostat detects the extra heat and turns on the water pump. This pumps water to the engine, cooling it again. Another thermostat controls the radiator cooling fan.

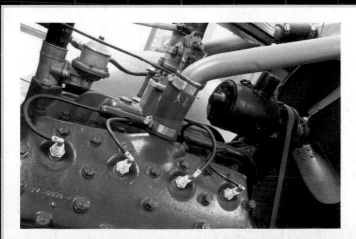

Intercooling

Some trucks have a device called an intercooler attached to the engine. Air from the turbocharger flows into the intercooler. The intercooler cools down the air. This makes the air more dense, which means that the same amount of air takes up less space. More air goes into the cylinders, which allows more fuel to be burned, giving the engine extra power.

Truck transmission

A truck's transmission connects the engine to the wheels. Its main part is the gearbox, which is used to change gear. A large truck may have 12 or more gears. Low gears are used for starting off and driving at low speeds. High gears are used for driving at faster speeds.

Drive shafts and axles

Drive shafts are rods that go from the gearbox to the wheels. The gearbox spins the drive shafts and the drive shafts turn the wheels. An axle is a drive shaft that powers two wheels on opposite sides of a truck. The cogs that turn an axle are called a differential.

Axle

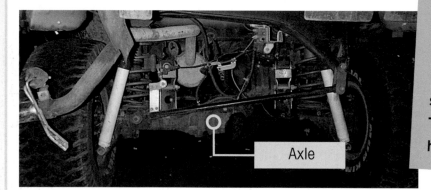

TECH FACT

Trucks that pull very heavy loads or work on rough ground need to travel at very low speeds. To do this, they have extra gears in each wheel hub. The gears make the wheels turn more slowly than the drive shaft. This system is called hub reduction.

Inside the gearbox

The gearbox allows the engine to turn the drive shafts at different speeds. The box is full of cogs of different sizes. Moving the gear lever makes different cogs interlock with each other. Each different combination of cogs is called a gear.

The clutch, gearbox and driveshafts

The transmission contains the clutch, the gearbox and the drive shafts. The engine has to be disconnected from the gearbox before the gears can be changed using the gear lever. This is done by the clutch. The gearbox turns the drive shafts at different speeds. The drive shafts turn the wheels.

Gear lever

I-TEC

Gearbox

Gearbox

Steering and brakes

A truck driver controls a truck with a steering wheel, pedals for the brakes, clutch and accelerator, and the gear lever. The steering wheel makes the front wheel turn from side to side. Trucks have powered steering to help the driver turn the wheels. The brakes slow the truck by stopping the wheels turning.

Discs and pads

There is a brake behind each wheel of a truck. A metal brake disc is connected to the drive shaft or axle. The disc turns with the wheel. When the driver presses the brake pedal, two pads squeeze the disc, which slows the wheel.

Air lines

Trailers have brakes, too. They are worked by air from the tractor unit. The air travels along air lines, or cables, which are connected when the trailer is attached to the tractor unit.

Air and hydraulics

Truck brakes are usually hydraulic. Hydraulic brakes use fluid to squeeze the brake pads together. Each brake has one or more brake cylinders with pistons inside. When the driver pushes the brake pedal, fluid is pushed into the cylinders. This pushes the piston, which pushes the pads onto the disc, stopping the wheel.

Brake disc

Wheel bolt

Brake pads

Wheel hub

Safety and comfort

A modern truck uses the latest technology to make it as safe as possible to drive. There are also features that protect car drivers, who are at risk of serious injury in an accident with a large truck. Truck drivers spend many hours in their cabs every day, so it is important for them to be comfortable. They have fully adjustable seats and air-conditioned cabs.

Seatbelts and airbags
Safety features in the cab include seatbelts and airbags. A seatbelt holds the driver in the driving seat during an accident. Airbags inflate instantly in an accident. They stop the driver from hitting the steering wheel or the sides of the cab.

Sleeper cabs
The biggest cabs are found on long-distance trucks. Their drivers can spend weeks on the road delivering their cargo. They have luxurious sleeper cabs, with a bed behind the seats, a washbasin, television, fridge and plenty of storage space.

TECH FACT

In many countries, truck drivers are allowed to drive only for a certain number of hours a day. Drivers must take regular breaks for sleep because driving while tired is dangerous. A device inside the cab called a tachograph (say TAKO–GRAAF) records when the truck is moving and when it is stopped.

Driver's seat

Overhead storage

Refrigerator

Microwave oven

Bed

Truck crash tests

New models of truck are tested to see what happens to them in an accident. The results of the tests show how safe the truck is for the driver. Tests are also carried out to see what happens if a car hits a truck. Bars on the chassis stop the car going under the truck.

Special trucks

Many types of truck are designed to perform special jobs, from fighting fires and collecting rubbish to racing around tracks and jumping over obstacles. These trucks normally have the same rigid chassis and cab as a cargo truck. The chassis and cab are built by a truck manufacturer, then a body is added to the chassis by a specialist truck maker.

Fork-life trucks

Fork-lift trucks (see opposite page) raise heavy loads onto high places. A fork slides underneath the load and supports its weight. The fork is attached to a carriage. The carriage is moved up and down a vertical mast using a hydraulic system.

TECH FACT

Specialized trucks often have machinery on board. For example, a dump truck has a lifting body, a garbage truck has a crusher, and a fire truck has a water tank and hoses. The machinery is operated by compressed air or hydraulics, and is powered by the truck's engine.

Concrete mixers

A concrete mixer carries wet concrete from a concrete plant to a building site. It mixes the ingredients together in its rotating drum. The drum spins backwards to make the concrete come out and down a delivery chute.

Monster trucks

Truck enthusiasts convert normal pick-up trucks into custom trucks by adding specialized parts. Monster trucks are custom trucks with high suspensions and giant tyres used to squash scrap cars.

Carriage

Fork

Hydraulic cylinder

Mast

Cab

Glossary

Accelerate
To speed up.

Articulated truck
A truck that bends in the middle, made up of a tractor unit that tows a trailer.

Chassis
The main structure of a truck, normally made up of two strong rails. It supports all the other parts of the truck.

Cog
A wheel with teeth around its edge.

Component
An object that is part of a larger, more complex machine.

Compressor
A machine that squeezes (compresses) air into a smaller space.

Cylinder
A space inside an engine where fuel burns.

Diesel engine
An engine that uses diesel (sometimes called DERV) as its fuel.

Exhaust
The parts of a truck that carry waste gases away from the engine.

Filter
A device that removes pieces of dirt from a liquid or a gas.

Fuel system
The parts of a truck that store fuel and pump it to the engine's cylinders.

Hub
The central part of a wheel, where it is attached to the truck.

Hydraulic
Describes a machine that has parts moved by liquid pumped along pipes.

Piston
Part of an engine that slides up and down a cylinder.

Pressure
The push made by air inside a tyre, or by gases inside an engine's cylinders.

Rigid truck
A truck that is not articulated. The chassis supports both the cab and the body.

Shock absorber
Part of a suspension that stops the suspension spring becoming too squashed or stretched.

Skid

When a truck slides along the road without one or more of the wheels turning. It happens when the tyres lose their grip on the road.

Suspension

Part of a truck that lets the wheels move up and down as the truck goes over bumps.

Tractor unit

The front part of an articulated truck, which contains the driver's cab and the engine.

Trailer

The rear part of an articulated truck, which is towed by a tractor unit.

Valve

Part of an engine that opens temporarily to let fuel into a cylinder, or exhaust gases out.

Further reading

Extreme Machines: Trucks
Ian Graham (Watts, 2006)

Usborne Beginners Trucks
Katie Daynes (Usborne, 2007)

Illustrated book of Trucks
Peter J Davies (Southwater, 2003)

Useful websites

www.macktrucks.com
Official site of Mack Trucks, an American truck manufacturer.

www.macktrucks.com/default.aspx?pageid=1443
Virtual tour of a Mack sleeper cab.

www.volvo.com/trucks/global/en-gb
Official site of Volvo trucks.

www.howstuffworks.com/flash/diesel.swf
Animation of how a diesel engine works.

www.aceshighmonstertruck.com
Home page of the Aces High monster truck.

Index